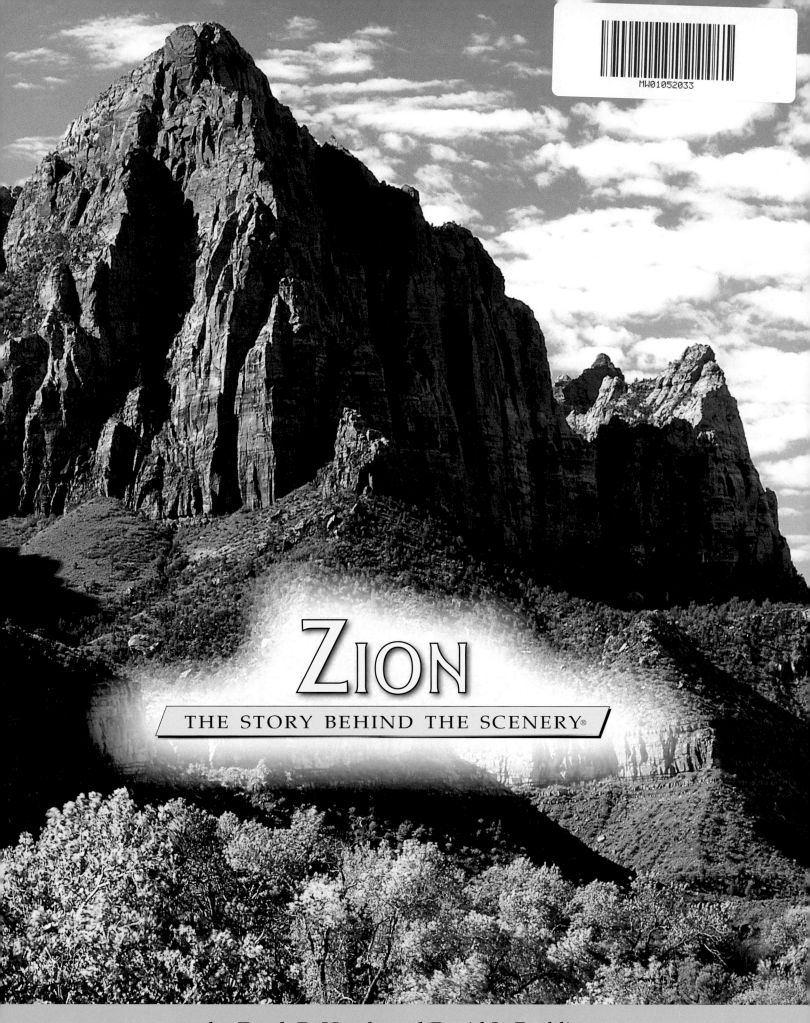

ZION

THE STORY BEHIND THE SCENERY®

by Frank R. Hayde and David L. Rachlis

FRANK R. HAYDE has worked as a ranger/naturalist at Zion, Redwood, and Canyonlands National Parks. DAVID RACHLIS worked as a ranger/naturalist at Zion National Park for nearly 10 years.

The colossal monoliths of Zion rise into the deep blue clarity
of a Utah sky. Like a soaring overture to a grand symphony,

sunrise on the Temples and Towers of the Virgin introduces a theme of might, color, and glory.

Zion is an ancient Hebrew word, originally used to describe a dry rocky place of holy sanctuary in ancient Israel. How fitting it is that today this same word should be associated with the magnificent towering cathedrals and temples of brightly colored stone we call Zion National Park.

The colorful rock layers of Zion were originally deposited in a series of ancient seas, swamps, rivers, forests, and a vast sand-dune desert. The remains of fossil fish, dinosaur tracks, and petrified wood all bear testimony to the various environments that have moved back and forth across the landscape through time.

Tectonic activity over the past several million years has abruptly uplifted these long-buried beds along the Hurricane Fault. The cutting power of the Virgin River and its tributaries erodes these rising layers into canyons and cliffs. The geologic processes that have created Zion are still actively at work and invite curiosity from all who view the spectacle.

Situated at the center of the Temple of Sinawava, the Pulpit towers over a congregation of cottonwoods in autumn along the Virgin River.

RICHARD CUMMINS

The Zion Story

The towering cliffs and deep canyons of Zion National Park give dramatic testament to the twin forces of uplift and erosion. Located along the southwestern edge of the Colorado Plateau, Zion presents some of the most colorfully spectacular scenery anywhere on earth. Shortly after it was first described and photographed in the mid-19th century, artists, photographers, and writers made the arduous journey to see for themselves this chromatic spectacle of the western American landscape. Today it is one of the most visited national parks in the world, its fame only growing in stature as new visitors continue to be awed by the majesty of this geologic wonderland.

With over 5,000 feet of vertical relief, Zion has a remarkable amount of plant and animal diversity within its boundaries. An excellent system of roads and trails makes it easy for the visitor to explore the large diversity of life zones found here. On the very top are forested plateaus offering wide-ranging vistas of distant mountains and canyons and the opportunity to view elk, deer, and—rarely—cougar. Deep down in the canyon bottoms, where direct sunlight shines only rarely, there are natural springs and seeps, which provide a habitat for ferns, grasses, flowers, and a variety of trees. The lowest sections of the park are occupied by dry desert badlands where salt-resistant shrubs and cactus share the blistered landscape with roadrunners, snakes, lizards, and coyotes. Except for the very highest sections of the park, Zion has a mild climate year-round that invites the exploration of its many wonders.

K.C. DenDooven
Publisher

The combination of extraordinary deposition and extraordinary erosion is displayed dramatically in the Narrows. Downstream, the river widens the canyon by cutting through the softer rocks that underlie the Navajo Sandstone. In the narrows the river is confined exclusively within the Navajo layer. This is a soft rock, but it has a uniformity of strength that causes it to erode evenly. Moving water cuts directly down through the entire 2,000-foot span of the sandstone. To look directly up at these walls while standing in the water that carved them is to experience the essence of Zion. It is, however, a trip that involves considerable risk, since narrow canyons are prone to flash flooding. A journey into the Narrows requires careful planning and proper equipment.

ED COOPER

***T*he smooth forms of Mt.** Abraham and Mt. Isaac rise from the floor of Birch Creek. These walls, seen from the Court of the Patriarchs overlook, are often compared to those in Yosemite Valley, due to their resemblance in texture and scale.

JEFF GNASS

***T*he patterns of Jurassic** wind lie frozen in stone. These "petrified" sand dunes form the Navajo Sandstone, which weathers into smooth slickrock. The sinuous patterns in the vicinity of the White Arch along the Zion-Mt. Carmel Highway are a favorite subject for roadside photographers.

Time and Layers

ERIC WUNROW

The geologic formations in Zion National Park preserve a record of changing landscapes and environments spanning 150 million years of the earth's history. The oldest sedimentary layer, the Toroweap limestone, dates from the close of the Permian period (270 million years ago), and the youngest layers represent the early Cretaceous (120 million years ago). The nearly 7,000 feet of sedimentary layers in the park were deposited in shallow ocean basins, lakes, rivers, forests, tidal flats, and a sand dune desert that created the famous Navajo Sandstone. The variety of environments is a result of the continuous northward movement of the North American landmass away from the equator, bringing about significant changes as it migrated through various climatic belts. Zion also contains geologically recent volcanic activity that dots the park with cinder cones and lava flows, some only thousands of years old.

The geological story of how the strata were laid down can best be told in sequence from the earliest to the latest times beginning with the lowest formations and proceeding upward.

The slot canyons of Zion are formed by the down-cutting action of water along major joints or fractures in the Navajo Sandstone. The abrasive force of periodic floods carrying sand, soil, and rock fragments scours the canyon bottoms and over time cuts deep notches into the surface of the formation. Visitors should use extreme caution when entering these narrow passages, especially during the summer when flash floods are a real possibility.

Crazy Quilt Mesa gets its name *from a combination of vertical grooves and horizontal layering that form on some north-facing exposures of Navajo sandstone. The horizontal lines represent the layers of sand that were deposited by wind during Jurassic time, while the vertical furrows are possibly fractures formed by heating and cooling.*

PERMIAN

The *Toroweap* and *Kaibab Formations* are both white to tan limestone layers, which were laid down in warm shallow seas on the western margin of a large continental landmass situated near the equator. Set astride an arid coastline not unlike the southwestern coast of modern-day Africa, this sea was abundant with corals, sea urchins, brachiopods, bryozoans, and sponges. Mollusk fossils occur more predominantly near the top of the Kaibab, possibly indicating a retreat of the sea as the water became shallower.

Both layers form only a small exposure in Zion and are located in the Kolob Canyons section only. The Kaibab and Toroweap are more noteworthy as the top two layers forming the rim of the Grand Canyon. The famous Virgin River Gorge along

"Zion...contains geologically recent volcanic activity..."

JOHN P. GEORGE

This view of Mt. Kinesava and the
Rockville Bench reveal in a glance
the principal sedimentary layers found in Zion National
Park. The tan caprock forming the lower cliff in the
foreground is the Shinarump Conglomerate, which is
part of the Chinle Formation. Above that are rounded
badland hills comprising the Petrified Forest member of
the Chinle Formation. Next are the sloping Moenave and
Kayenta Formations, which sit beneath the massive
vertical cliffs of the Navajo Sandstone.

The Grand

Zion is located at the midway point in a series of stair-stepped plateaus known as the Grand Staircase. Faulting associated with Great Basin tectonics has underridden and uplifted the massive western edge of the Colorado Plateau, creating the High Plateaus section. From the alpine forests of Cedar Breaks and Bryce Canyon, the land breaks off to the south dropping nearly 8,000 feet in 200 miles to the very bottom of the Grand Canyon. The

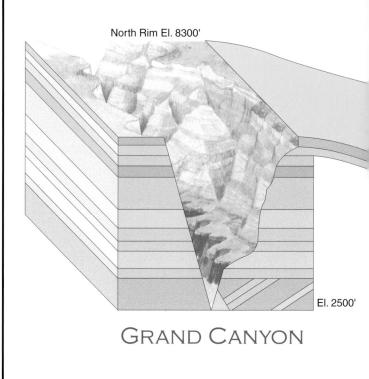

North Rim El. 8300'

El. 2500'

GRAND CANYON

Interstate Highway 15 south of St. George is where these layers are best displayed, forming the dramatic steep canyon walls on this scenic route.

TRIASSIC

The *Moenkopi Formation* records a tidal environment along a very flat coastal plain and is a continuation of the shallow marine setting that laid down the Kaibab. This colorful banded formation contains red, brown, tan, and white beds nearly 1,800 feet thick. Mainly composed of limestone, shale, and gypsum, this relatively soft formation

Staircase

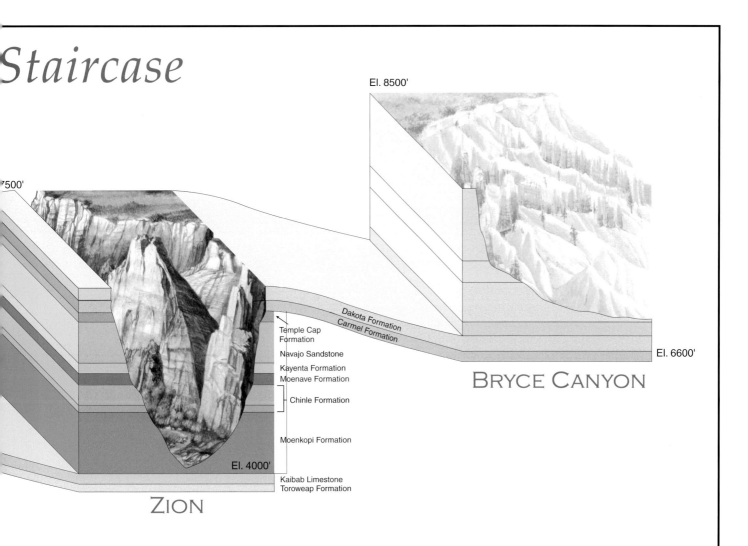

El. 8500'

'500'

Dakota Formation
Carmel Formation

Temple Cap Formation

Navajo Sandstone

Kayenta Formation

Moenave Formation

Chinle Formation

Moenkopi Formation

El. 4000'

Kaibab Limestone
Toroweap Formation

ZION

El. 6600'

BRYCE CANYON

corresponding variety of climatic conditions created by this great range in elevation is astounding, encompassing every major life zone found in North America.. Many of these uplifted plateaus rise high enough for sufficient snow accumulation to provide for year-round streams and rivers, which can then cut into the rock layers below creating canyons. The Virgin River, which is carving Zion Canyon, drops an

astonishing 8,000 feet in a little over 160 miles, giving it one of the steepest stream gradients on the continent, 50 feet a mile! The sedimentary layers exposed in the Grand Staircase record nearly 2 billion years of the earth's history.

DICK BEASLEY

easily erodes into slopes, mounds, and short cliffs. The Moenkopi is most easily seen on the main western approach to Zion along Utah Highway 9 near the town of Virgin.

By the late Triassic the shallow marine environment of the Moenkopi began to give way to continental river sedimentation, possibly triggered by mountain building to the south and east. The *Chinle Formation* contains two members, the *Shinarump Conglomerate*—which forms prominent white to tan cliffs resting on top of the Moenkopi—and the rounded purplish gray bad-

lands of the *Petrified Forest* member. The Shinarump is a pebbly conglomerate deposited in a river system that carried material down from a mountainous source area speculated to have been in Colorado and New Mexico. The Petrified Forest member is composed of purple, gray, and white shale that contains abundant fossilized wood fragments. The purple coloration of the rock is due to bentonite, a decomposed volcanic material, most probably derived from ash clouds emanating from nearby volcanoes. These hot clouds of volcanic material spewed from cinder cones and vents and

A *variety of erosional forms in different*
layers can be seen along the Chinle Trail.
The soft purplish shale of the Petrified Forest member of the Chinle Formation, in the foreground, is soft and
composed of bentonite clay, which swells when wet and shrinks when it dries, causing it to slump. Above that is
the blocky brick-like Moenave Formation, which lies beneath the sloping orange and red Kayenta Formation.
The cliffs of Navajo Sandstone looming above form the ramparts of Mt. Kinesava.

over time slowly killed off a vast coniferous forest. Minerals of silica in this volcanic material impregnated the streams and swamps the dead trees lay in and over time replaced the original plant structure, forming petrified wood.

The Chinle also contains concentrations of uranium, which were mined extensively throughout the Colorado Plateau during the Cold War period for the production of atomic weapons grade ore. The Chinle Formation can be seen in the brightly colored slopes and low cliffs in and around the town of Springdale at the mouth of Zion Canyon.

JURASSIC

Above the Chinle is the early Jurassic *Moenave Formation*, which is composed of three members (bottom to top): *Dinosaur Canyon, Whitmore Point,* and *Springdale Sandstone*. The Moenave preserves lake, river, and flood plain sediments deposited in both high and low energy stream environments. The bottom two members consist of reddish and purple siltstones and sandstones that have been found to contain fossilized fish remains resembling the modern-day sturgeon. The Springdale

Sandstone is a stream deposit, with channel fills of cross-bedded sandstone that are separated by layers of floodplain mudstones. It forms a prominent cliff face 75 to 150 feet high, which can easily be seen along the main park road in the vicinity of the South Entrance Station.

The *Kayenta Formation*, in most places less than 200 feet thick, forms the steep sloping red to maroon colored rocks between the top of the Springdale Sandstone and the bottom of the Navajo Sandstone. The Kayenta records more deposition in rivers, lakes, and swamps, where dinosaur footprints and trackways are fairly common. These three-toed reptiles walked upright and were most probably meat eaters. They left their tracks in the muddy swamps and playas of these coastal Jurassic lowlands. These prints can be found along the trail in the Left Fork of North Creek in the north central part of the park.

The continent continued to drift northwestward and by the middle of the Jurassic, sand dunes and a desert environment overtook the swampy plains and began forming what is now the most famous rock layer in Zion, the *Navajo Sandstone*. Often compared to the modern Sahara, the Navajo desert spread across major portions of Utah, Arizona, Nevada, Colorado, and Wyoming. Here sands accumulated to average depths of over 1,000 feet, much higher than any found on earth today. Where Zion is today, the sands reached their maximum thickness of over 3,000 feet, resulting in the highest sandstone cliffs in the world.

dunes. Today these solid and impermeable rock masses form springs high up in the middle sections of the Navajo Sandstone. The Canyon Overlook Trail offers an excellent example.

The *Temple Cap Formation* is so named because it forms a conspicuous capping layer over the Navajo Sandstone, most famously at the East and

In Hidden Canyon one can find good examples in the Navajo Sandstone of what is called cavernous weathering. This type of erosion is caused by a lack of cementing agents in the rock. In most cases it occurs where calcite has been taken out by water moving through the rock, leaving cavities behind that eventually are exposed in the canyon walls.

Crossbedding is one of the most conspicuous features of Navajo Sandstone. It is a record in the rock, which reveals the shifting winds that carried enormous volumes of sand through here during the Jurassic. The sloping 30-degree angle of the lines shows the direction in which the dunes were blowing. Where these lines change direction is simply where the wind changed direction 180 million years ago. Visitors traveling along the Zion-Mt. Carmel Highway encounter these diagonal lines in the rock and are intrigued by the patterns.

The Navajo desert also contained many oases, where fine-grained silt and mudstones collected in small shallow depressions scattered among the

West Temples of the main canyon. This yellow to brown mudstone represents a change to stream deposition before dunes again returned. The red streaks found on many of the higher cliffs in Zion Canyon are a direct result of this formation leaching its iron-rich content downward onto the surface of the Navajo. The Altar of Sacrifice is named because this color resembles dripping blood.

The *Carmel Formation* is a limestone laid down in a shallow sea at the close of Jurassic time. This light tan to gray rock contains abundant marine fossils, including crinoids, clams, and oysters. Along Clear Creek near the East Entrance Station, many boulders in the stream bottom preserve outstanding specimens. The calcium carbonate in this limestone precipitates downward through solution, infiltrating the Navajo Sandstone below. Along with iron oxide, calcium carbonate cements the sand grains together.

Within the park, most of the rocks that once lay above the Carmel have been worn away. Concluding Zion's sequence of sedimentary layers is the *Dakota Formation*. On top of Zion's highest peak, Horse Ranch Mountain, we find a small remnant of this much wider-ranging rock type. Just as the top layers at the Grand Canyon form a

*T*he Great Arch of Zion is a wonderful example of the intermediate stage in the creation of a freestanding natural arch. The sandstone along the canyon wall is divided into linear slabs by joints in the rock, which separate from the cliff face when water penetrates them and begins to erode a larger gap. Over time large segments will weather out behind the arched slab allowing it to eventually stand alone.

ED COOPER

-14-

bridge to Zion's lowest strata, the Dakota represents the connection to Bryce Canyon where this layer is also found.

Faulting, uplift, and volcanic activity followed the era of sedimentation. The basalt flows and associated cones found in Zion represent material that is much younger, having been extruded in only the last few million years. It is much more mineral rich and thus more resistant to erosion. It forms a caprock over many of the softer and much older sedimentary layers below.

COLORATION

The bold and striking red and orange coloration of the rock layers is what draws many visitors to the Colorado Plateau. The main ingredient in creating these impressive hues is iron oxide. This plentiful mineral is locally abundant in rocks from the Triassic through the Tertiary. Just as old metal displays red rust when exposed to the elements, rocks containing iron oxide can range from crimson to cream in coloration, depending on the concentration of iron present. There are still many debates among geologists as to whether or not a particular formation contained its current content of iron oxide when it was originally deposited or if it came later when water percolated through carrying minerals in solution. Sometimes it is a combination of both processes.

In Zion Canyon the Navajo Sandstone is white on top and more red and orange colored towards the bottom, while at the Kolob Canyons the Navajo is solidly red from top to bottom. The difference is that in the Kolob Canyons the rocks have been so recently uplifted that the overlying layers have not been worn away by erosion. They act as a protective barrier above the Navajo keeping water from permeating it, thus preserving the red coloration. In Zion Canyon a more advanced stage of erosion has stripped away the overlying strata, allowing water to leach out the red coloration and leave behind white-topped canyon walls.

Dark black streaks along vertical cracks and below hanging valleys contain tannic acid from coniferous trees. Some black areas found along canyon walls are called desert varnish. This is a process whereby organic and inorganic forces combine to create a manganese oxide crust. It takes a very long time for this material to form and was the favored medium of petroglyph art for many centuries.

Black volcanic rock can be found over a wide section of Zion. These geologically much younger igneous rocks get their distinctive black coloration from the rich mineral content found in these basalts. If you break a piece open, it reveals a light gray crystalline rock that is full of small air bubbles. Some is so vesicular that it approaches the consistency of pumice. This material slowly oozed across the brightly colored sandstone and shale. Today it appears as a coating of chocolate icing on a giant slab of layer cake. A great place to see these juxtaposing beds is along Utah Highway 9 between Coal Pits Wash and Virgin, Utah.

TOM DANIELSEN

The red streaks on the Altar of Sacrifice are derived from iron oxide deposits that were weathered out of the overlying Temple Cap Formation and carried over the surface of the cliff by water. As the water evaporates, the thin veneer of red coloration is left behind on the stark white cliffs of Navajo Sandstone.

JEFF GNASS

Calm beauty belies the Virgin River's aggressive role in the carving of Zion Canyon. Periodic flooding transforms this seemingly placid stream into an abrasive erosional force, which has denuded the surrounding rock into remnant towers such as Angel's Landing, one of Zion's most famous landmarks.

The Virgin River is one of the steepest in North America

A Land Is Uplifted— A Canyon Is Carved

Zion National Park lies at the southwestern edge of the Colorado Plateau, where it makes contact with the tectonically active faulting of the Great Basin. Immediately west of Zion the continent has been in a steady process of expansion, whereby California, Nevada, and Utah are gradually being pulled apart in an east to west direction. This continental stretching has created enormous fissures in the earth's crust called faults, which are breaking the land into a series of north-south trending plateaus and valleys. This area is known as the High Plateaus section of the Colorado Plateau, home of Zion, Bryce Canyon, and Cedar Breaks, comprising some of the most spectacular geologic scenery on earth.

Zion is located adjacent to the rapidly rising Hurricane Fault. This active fault zone originates in the Grand Canyon and runs in a north-south direction for 160 miles and is the southwestern boundary of the Colorado Plateau. It is the relentless upward force along this fault that has brought about the spectacular scenery we see today at Zion and surrounding areas. In the Kolob Canyons section of the park, located along the trace of the fault, visitors can marvel at beds of massive 2,000-foot-thick red Navajo Sandstone that have literally been thrust straight up out of the ground.

The sheer height of the topography in Zion is due in part to the fact that uplift augments the erosive power of local streams to cut and carry the massive rock material away. Without regional uplift, the scourings the land receives from intermittent rains and snowmelt would be insufficient to have carved this scenery so dramatically. In

JOHN ELK III

***T**his great bend in Zion Canyon as seen from the East Rim Trail is a spectacular example of canyon erosion on a grand scale. Here the Virgin River has carved a meander into the horizontal layers of the Kayenta and Navajo Formations. This sharp curve in the streambed is believed by some geologists to have been formed when the Virgin flowed across a flat flood plain prior to regional uplift and was carved into the rock as the land rose. Note that the river is running full of silt following a flash flood.*

southwestern Utah the earth's crust is especially thin from the stretching action of the continent previously mentioned. This creates added buoyancy for the overlying rock, which allows it to rise even faster than it would if the crust were denser.

Locally the Hurricane Fault has pushed the land up over 10,000 feet in the last 3 to 5 million years, forming the steep western edge of the Markagunt Plateau. (*Markagunt* is the Paiute word for "highland of trees.") From the top of Brian Head Peak (11,304 feet) one can look south past the spectacular amphitheatre of Cedar Breaks National Monument and beyond to the flat and forested expanse of the Kolob Terrace into which the canyons of Zion are carved. This stair-stepped terracing of the land continues eastward where the Paunsaugunt Plateau (where Bryce Canyon National Park is located), the Aquarius Plateau, and the Table Cliffs all share the same pattern of headward erosion.

These plateaus comprise the top of a local geographic feature known as the Grand Staircase. These uplifted plateaus send rivers south out of snow-capped highlands, carving spectacular canyons as they flow down into the depths of the Colorado River. When these streams cut through the Navajo Sandstone layer, they create deep and narrow slot canyons. Carved by the year-round flow of the Virgin River, the 14-mile Zion Narrows is the largest and most spectacular example of this phenomenon.

In the vicinity of Zion three distinct geographic regions meet in transition. On the east, the Hurricane Fault and its associated plateaus represent the western edge of the Colorado Plateau province. Immediately west, the Pine Valley

Mountains, an intrusive body of igneous rock, mark the beginning of the Great Basin province, which stretches 500 miles west from the Hurricane Fault to the Sierra Mountains in California. Just south of Zion the land drops off into the stark vastness of the Mojave Desert with its distinctive geology, plants, and animals. Geologists refer to this border area as the Basin and Range–Colorado Plateau Transition Zone. As a result, Zion contains many overlapping characteristics of the various geographic provinces it borders.

ED COOPER

Weeping Rock is one of several famous springs located in Zion Canyon, all of which owe their origin to the contact line between the Navajo Sandstone and the underlying Kayenta Formation. The Navajo is very porous and contains a large amount of water that is pulled downward by gravity. When this flowing water finally reaches the less permeable Kayenta layer, it is forced out laterally to form springs and seeps. Kayenta is a Navajo word that means "place of the springs."

Along the Virgin River in upper Zion Canyon one can view the softer shale of the Kayenta Formation cutting back more rapidly under the more resistant Navajo Sandstone, creating large overhanging blocks. These jointed slabs eventually break off of the canyon wall and crash violently down, creating huge clouds of sand and dust.

JOHN P. GEORGE

Regional Setting

The Grand Staircase is an evocative name describing a series of terraced plateaus rising from the depths of the Grand Canyon. Starting from the right of the diagram with the Kaibab Uplift, we move upward through the Belted and Vermilion Cliffs consisting of soft multi-colored sedimentary layers. The towering sandstones of the White Cliffs are best exemplified in the high canyon walls of Zion and Capitol Reef. Cretaceous seafloor deposits make up the majority of the Grey Cliffs, which are covered with vegetation and are thus partially obscured to the traveler. At the top are the Pink Cliffs, famously presented at Bryce Canyon and Cedar Breaks.

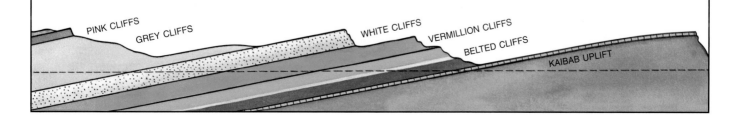

PINK CLIFFS
GREY CLIFFS
WHITE CLIFFS
VERMILLION CLIFFS
BELTED CLIFFS
KAIBAB UPLIFT

THE LAYERS ARE EXPOSED

The Virgin River, draining a large highland area, flows south out of the Markagunt Plateau from an elevation of over 10,000 feet. It then proceeds to drop nearly 8,000 feet in only 160 miles, emptying into the Colorado River at Lake Mead. This stream gradient of between 50 to 70 feet to the mile is one of the steepest in North America, carrying away more than a million tons of rock waste each year. The elements necessary for active, rapid erosion are here.

Torrential flooding during the monsoon season transforms the shallow clear waters of the Virgin into what some refer to as a red ribbon of liquid sandpaper. Because most of the surrounding soil is simply bare rock, the water runs off very quickly, filling the streams and canyons, and sweeping everything in its path toward the Virgin River.

Imagine a churning conveyor belt of boulders, trees, foam, and debris. The immediate effects of such flooding are readily apparent to any witness. For the river to go from 40 cubic feet per second (CFS) to 4,000 CFS in less than an hour is a stunning sight of canyon creation. Stream channels are altered, new banks are deposited, and vegetation is destroyed.

Facilitating the erosional process are the cracks or joints that cleave the cliffs. Since water naturally flows into cracks, these joints determine the configuration of most of the drainages. Freezing and thawing causes joints to expand and contract, widening the canyon as entire slabs of rock fall away. Each of Zion's rock layers erodes differently. Chemical composition determines the hardness of rock, which in turn determines the rate of erosion.

BRITT PIERSON

A hanging valley is a tributary that ends high above the floor of the main canyon. Since the Navajo walls are nearly vertical, these features are very impressive. The hanging valleys develop because the tributaries cannot keep pace with the erosion rate of the Virgin River. If they were projected out into the main canyon, the hanging valleys would locate earlier levels of the Virgin River hundreds of feet above its present course.

ED COOPER

*J*oints and cracks on the face of the Sentinel are responsible for the many loose slabs of protruding rock that appear to be falling away before our very eyes. As the river carries away more material the canyon widens, causing the walls to sag inward towards the empty space. These onion-like layers or slabs eventually weaken their grip to the main wall and fall.

In Zion Canyon, the most impressive rock layer is the 3,000-foot-thick Navajo Sandstone. This white, orange, and red colored rock dominates the scenery. Navajo Sandstone erodes into the slot canyons, arches, and smooth slickrock that millions of visitors travel to see each year. Many people are surprised to see trees growing straight out of the rock. The porosity of this loosely cemented sandstone enables it to retain a tremendous amount of water. As tree roots grow inside the rock, cracks expand and slabs fall away, contributing to the cycle of erosion.

The water contained in the Navajo Sandstone continues to migrate downward until it reaches

"Facilitating the erosional process are the cracks or joints that cleave the cliffs."

LIN ALDER

Many visitors are curious about the difference between plateaus, mesas, and buttes. Plateaus are large landforms, which eventually erode into mesas, like those seen here in the lighted foreground. Smaller still are buttes, isolated by four steep sides and representing the later stage of the erosive process. From left to right we see the conical Crater Hill, the flat tabletop of the Rockville Mesa, and the heights of Mt. Kinesava.

the less permeable Kayenta Formation. This layer, formed of tightly packed clay minerals, diverts the water laterally, forming springs. Weeping Rock, the Emerald Pools, and the springs along the Riverside Walk are all a result of contact between two different types of rock. Recent studies of these year-round springs reveal the rate of time it takes for the water to pass through the Navajo Sandstone to be thousands of years. Imagine standing underneath Weeping Rock and touching water that first fell as rain during Medieval times. Because the water is so well insulated in the rock, it maintains a constant temperature of about 62 degrees Fahrenheit.

SENTINEL SLIDE AND LAKE

Like flash floods, catastrophic landslides have played an important role in the overall erosion of Zion Canyon. The Sentinel Slide dammed the river and created a lake upstream in which clay, silt, and sand beds were deposited. This slide occurred approximately 5,000 years ago and can still be readily seen from the lower part of the Zion Canyon Scenic Drive. Just below the towering

Sentinel Peak, massive mounds of broken bedrock cover this section of the canyon. The river ultimately cut a channel through the slide dam, draining the lake. Scientists suggest that at one time the lake was 125 feet deep and extended north to the base of Angel's Landing.

Sections of the Sentinel Slide still continue to slump and occasionally impede the river. In 1995 one such slump dammed the Virgin for several hours until the river carved itself a new channel right through the Zion Canyon Scenic Drive. This section of Zion Canyon is the most actively unstable, and it is reasonable to expect that it will provide even more dramatic geologic events in the future.

VOLCANISM

Zion's geology is most readily associated with the cycle of deposition, uplift, and erosion of sedimentary rock. We now turn to the lesser known but no less interesting volcanic features found

In April 1995 a major slump occurred in the soft unconsolidated sand slope along the western bank of the Virgin River. A section of the Zion Canyon Scenic Drive was destroyed after the river backed up and carved a new channel through the pavement, necessitating reconstruction. This unstable area is prone to landslides, which also dammed the river in 1923 and 1941. The Virgin River is constantly cutting along the edge of this talus, especially during periods of flash flooding, when high volumes of water sweep through and undercut the slope.

JEFF GNASS

throughout the park. Zion is part of a larger regional geologic zone known as the Western Grand Canyon Basaltic Field. Here the earth's crust has been fractured in a series of north-south trending faults where volcanic activity is fairly common. These deep fissures allow magma to rise from within the crust and extrude upon the surface.

Throughout this region these incongruously black, blocky, and lightly weathered rocks evoke curiosity. Because magma is so close to the surface in southern Utah, it is considered by many geologists to still be in an active phase. Renewed activity could return at any time. The most recent volcanism occurred less than a thousand years ago. Zion contains cinder cones, lava flows, and inverted valleys.

Three well-defined cinder cones exist within the park's boundaries: Firepit Knoll, Spendlove Knoll, and Crater Hill. All dating from no earlier than 1.4 million years ago, these peculiar features are located along the Cougar Mountain Fault zone. This linear fracture has resulted in a pronounced cluster of volcanic activity in Zion, which can be easily seen from Utah Highway 9 near Coalpits Wash and along the Kolob Terrace Road. Look for these rounded cones with their conspicuous 30-degree slopes appearing strangely exotic above the surrounding sedimentary terrain.

Associated with these lava cones are six basaltic flows that filled stream channels and covered the landscape in locally deep accumulations of

*V*olcanic cones similar in age, composition, and structure to the one pictured here dot the landscape of the greater Zion region. These recently formed features attest to the active geologic forces still simmering beneath the locally thin crust of the Western Grand Canyon Basaltic Field, which stretches over a wide area of southern Utah and northern Arizona.

DAVID MUENCH

CAROL POLICH

*I*ron-rich caprock acts like a hard hat to protect what it covers. Here it has prevented the underlying rock from being eroded away. The result is a spire-shaped form known as a hoodoo.

porous black lava rock. The flows in Zion were usually 10 to 40 feet thick, with deeper accumulations filling canyons. When this material cooled, forming rock, its rich mineral composition rendered it much harder than the softer underlying sedimentary rock.

When these flows emptied into an established watercourse, they would cool off and solidify into the new canyon bottom. Over time they became what geologists call inverted valleys. By cutting around the margins of the lava flow into the softer adjacent sedimentary layers, the streams eventually cut deep canyons, leaving the former streambed stranded high above. Thus what was once the bottom of the valley now comprises its top. Zion contains several classic stages of this process in the drainages of North Creek.

Zion's geology is perhaps most remarkable for its simplicity. Who would ever expect that such a geologic showcase would be relatively easy to understand? This is not to say that the geology of Zion is *normal*. As we see, it is quite exceptional. Yet few places illustrate the basics as well as Zion: deposition, uplift, and erosion. For this reason it is the ideal place to launch a study of geology. Anyone willing to scratch the surface is rewarded with concepts that can be applied all over the earth.

SUGGESTED READING

FILLMORE, ROBERT. *The Geology of the Parks, Monuments, and Wildlands of Southern Utah*. Salt Lake City: University of Utah Press, 2000.

HAMILTON, WAYNE L. *The Sculpturing of Zion*. Springdale, Utah: Zion Natural History Association, 1995.

STOKES, WILLIAM LEE. *Geology of Utah*. Salt Lake City, Utah: Utah Museum of Natural History, 1986.

UTAH GEOLOGICAL ASSOCIATION. *Geology of Utah's Parks and Monuments*. Salt Lake City, Utah: Utah Geological Association, 2000.

Icon of Zion's east side, **Checkerboard**
Mesa is a bold example of what the erosive
cycle can achieve. Visitors and geologists alike puzzle at this strange weathering of Navajo
Sandstone. Normal surface weathering takes on a more irregular pattern, but here the vertical
furrows are evenly spaced and are approximately the same depth. Furthermore,
checkerboarding occurs only on north-facing slopes. This uniformity is not yet fully understood,
but most probably is the result of a cycle of freezing and thawing. At a glance, these
markings appear to have been carved by a guiding hand.

ED COOPER

A seed sprouts on sandstone,
impressing us with its improbable pursuit.
We should not doubt it or pity it,
for it flourishes, finding here all that
it needs to grow and bear seeds of its own.

Flora at Zion

RICHARD CUMMINS

On Zion's east side, ponderosa pines grow out of seemingly barren rock. The water-rich Navajo Sandstone compensates for scarce precipitation, allowing these trees to survive where they normally could not. As the tree roots expand in the rock, cracks widen opening the way for more water and subsequent erosion.

JOHN P. GEORGE

Much of the scarce rainwater reaches the base of the Navajo Sandstone where it is forced out by less permeable rock, creating springs and hanging gardens. These lush zones of verdant green provide a lesson in how life thrives whenever ample supplies of water are available. The conifers shown in both of these photos owe their existence to the porous, sponge-like Navajo Sandstone, which allows them to grow at elevations much lower than their normal range.

JOHN ELK III

The razor-sharp leaves of the Utah yucca have the dual purpose of protecting the plant and channeling rain drops down towards its thirsty roots. Each spring a set of beautiful flowers adorns the narrow stalk. This strong and fibrous plant was utilized in the manufacture of sandals, rope, soap, baskets, and ladders.

A Desert Garden?

With over 5,000 feet of vertical relief, Zion provides a multitude of botanical habitats. Low-elevation deserts rise through several life zones, climaxing into luxuriant forests. Along canyon bottoms, a sun-baked cactus grows perhaps only a few feet from moisture-loving maidenhair fern. Cottonwoods and other deciduous trees plot the waterways, which are flanked by semi-arid slopes of pinyon and juniper. Next come thickets of oak and maple, which eventually transition into open stands of ponderosa pine. Higher yet is a mixed-conifer forest interspersed with groves of quaking aspen. Colorful wildflowers blossom at all elevations from spring through fall.

Another important factor in Zion's plant life is its location at the convergence of three separate geographic provinces. Plant species from the Great Basin, Colorado Plateau, and Mojave Desert coexist here. This combination of unique geographical factors is responsible for Zion possessing the highest diversity of plant species in the state of Utah.

Spring lines in the canyon provide another unique set of conditions requiring specialized plant adaptations. The hanging gardens of Zion contain ferns, horsetail, columbine, and thick moss, reminding us of places far, far away from the desert.

The springs of Zion support hanging garden microhabitats. Plants seen here include ferns, mosses, reed grasses, and flowers. Visitors are often surprised to find plants more commonly associated with the lush Pacific Northwest than the arid Southwest.

LIN ALDER

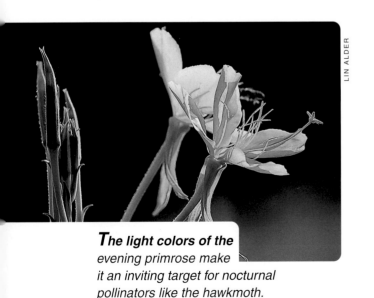

The light colors of the evening primrose make it an inviting target for nocturnal pollinators like the hawkmoth.

CAROL POLICH

JOHN P. GEORGE

Clusters of Indian paintbrush festoon the slickrock country of Zion in early spring and again in the fall.

C Cactus provide us with a lesson in conservation for survival. The average American uses 140 gallons of water each day. That amount of water would last a cactus more than 50 years. Shallow, widespread roots allow cacti to capture rainfall that runs off into sandy, non-absorbent soils. Tough, insulating skin and pulpy stems retain the precious water and sustain the cactus through periods of drought when the plant will shrink and shrivel as its reserves are used. When rains come again the succulent stems will swell as their reserves are replenished. The absence of leaves is another water-saving adaptation. In place of leaves the cactus has its spines, which protect the plant and provide a small but significant amount of shade.

GAIL BANDINI

JOHN P. GEORGE

The bright coloration of prickly pear *cactus flowers attracts many insects that fertilize the plants by transferring pollen from male to female organs. Here one can see the male anthers surrounding the female stigma, which has been successfully coated with yellow pollen grains. Specks of pollen are also visible clinging to the petals.*

Beavertail is a variety of prickly pear, which grows low to the ground and generally lacks large, prominent spines. Instead, it has clusters of hairlike barbs called glochids. Beware, for these tiny points are as menacing and painful as large spines and even harder to remove.

Perhaps more so than even the rose, the cactus exemplifies delicate beauty contrasted with thorny resistance. In April and May Zion is a showcase of blossoming prickly pear (shown here), hedgehog, and cholla cacti. Notice where the petals have expired atop the egg-shaped fruits. These fruits will ripen to a dark red by late summer. These "cactus apples" make a tasty treat for many mammals.

Overleaf: A cold vaporous mist clings to the treetops along Oak Creek. Pacific storms in the winter and spring provide most of the year's available supply of water by building a snowpack in the high country. Zion Canyon averages 14.5 inches of precipitation annually. Photo by Michael Plyler.

Zion contains the classic array of animal species long associated with the desert Southwest. Coyote, raven, rattlesnake, and cougar are but a few of the animals found here.

Animals of Zion

DIANE ENSIGN

Records show Meleagris gallopava *present in Zion Canyon in the early 20th century. A long absence ensued until they returned in the mid-1990s. Wild turkeys now thrive and are easily admired along the Zion Canyon Scenic Drive. Here the male, or gobbler, exhibits his red beard. He will prance with fanned tail feathers to impress the hens of his harem.*

Critters at Zion

A chuckwalla lizard patrols the warm desert only a few miles from a bull elk bugling in a snowy forest. While many animals stay within their own distinct habitats, others cross back and forth, flourishing in all of Zion's diverse domains. A great many species mix in the restricted space of the main canyon, with natural rhythms preventing the chaos that might arise from such crowding. Some species are active during the day (diurnal), others at night (nocturnal). These rotating schedules allow animals to occupy the same sites without interfering with each other. Some animals that are diurnal in other parts of the country are nocturnal in the desert Southwest—an adaptation to the summer heat. Some local wildlife have undergone adaptations that are specific to the Virgin River watershed. One, the Zion snail, is so well adapted to unique conditions in Zion Canyon that it is found nowhere else on earth.

JOHN P. GEORGE

Of Zion's larger mammals, mule deer are the most conspicuous. *An obvious contrast exists between the herd in Zion Canyon, and the mule deer of the high country. While the canyon deer seem accustomed to humans and poorly nourished, those on the plateau appear shy and much healthier. The great sandstone cliffs act as a divider and limit contact between the two herds.*

This golden-mantled ground squirrel is easily confused with the chipmunk but it lacks the characteristic facial striping. Small rodents occupy a variety of habitats in Zion. Many visitors are tempted to feed these "cute" animals, not realizing that they are likely to bite and that they could become sick from human food.

DAVID WEINSTEIN

Although mice can be difficult to identify, the larger ears of the pinyon mouse help distinguish it from the others. Large ears are a common desert adaptation among mammals. They act like radiators, allowing hot blood to circulate through the thin membrane of the ear and come into contact with the cooler outside air.

JOHN P. GEORGE

JOHN P. GEORGE

This small amphibian is often mistaken for a large mammal. In the early spring the canyon tree frog emits a mating call that sounds remarkably similar to the braying sound that sheep make. Many visitors report hearing a wild ram and are surprised to learn that such a big sound would come from such a little frog.

FRANK S. BALTHIS

In the early part of the 20th century a local hunter named Uncle Jim Owen killed 730 cougars in southwest Utah. Even park rangers had contempt for these animals and killed them in order for deer to flourish. Cougars persisted, however, and their numbers are now on the rebound. Today's rangers revere the cougar and hope for more predation on the overpopulated deer herd.

A Beaver Cuts a Tree – Good or Bad?

In the 1920s and 1930s the National Park Service armored the banks of the Virgin River with wire-covered rocks to prevent the river channel from shifting and wreaking havoc with the infrastructure of Zion Canyon. This modification of the floodplain ecosystem made it harder for cottonwood trees to regenerate because it acted to drain away water that otherwise would be available to sustain new growth. Currently there is an overstory of mature trees, with no younger trees to take their place. In their search for tender young cottonwood tissue, beaver are believed to be cutting the older trees to stimulate the growth of new shoots. In the process they are unwittingly destroying older trees that they would not normally cut. The park service is looking for ways to re-connect the river to the floodplain and re-store a balance between the beaver and the riparian environment.

FRANK S. BALTHIS

ERIC WUNROW

With food sources such as fish and rabbit readily available, the bald eagle finds a suitable wintering ground in Zion where weather rarely affects food supply. An immature bald eagle may reach three years and a full wingspan of six to seven feet before it acquires the white head and tail of an adult. Other notable birds of prey at Zion are the peregrine falcon, the Mexican spotted owl, and the California condor.

JOHN P. GEORGE

The white-crowned sparrow, which arrives towards the end of the year, is a favorite for those participating in the annual Christmas bird count. It is perhaps the most abundant of many seasonal migrants to the relatively warm winters of Zion. Birders are drawn to Zion in the winter because it attracts a wide variety of species including waterfowl and raptors.

The western bluebird delights the eye with its brilliant coloration. These birds often nest in old woodpecker holes. They are year-round residents of Zion.

Easily recognized by its prominent crest, the Steller's jay has been described as the beautiful bird with the ugly voice. Listen for their signature squawk in the pine and fir forests of Zion's high country. It is a warning not to leave food out for these clever campsite robbers.

Not to be confused with its cousin the crow, the raven is a huskier bird with shaggy throat feathers, a thicker bill, and a wedge-shaped tail. The two species have divided the range of the continent nicely, with crows dominating the east and ravens the west. Both are, along with jays and magpies, members of the family Corvidae—a group known for their raucous calls and overt intelligence. Ravens are superb flyers. They are comfortable soaring like a hawk, diving like a falcon, or tumbling like an acrobat. Like the crow, ravens walk instead of hop and unlike most other birds, mate for life. Despite this, they have a reputation of evil ways, no doubt due in part to their omnivorous appetite that includes crops and garbage. Fortunately for us, they also devour scads of insects and rodents.

Kolob is a word from the Book of Mormon meaning the star nearest the throne of God, signifying a high, exalted place.

The Kolob

Since 1937 the Kolob Canyons have been protected as a westward extension of the high-walled cliff formations characteristic of Zion. In 1972 a new road penetrated this trackless wilderness, opening it to closer examination. Despite its easy access off of Interstate 15 (Exit 40), this district still receives relatively few visitors. Those taking the time to explore this unique tract will discover a splendor that is arguably more magnificent than that found in the main canyon. Here along the Hurricane Fault the Navajo Sandstone has been uplifted in dramatic fashion. The distance between rock formations has also been greatly compressed. For example, in the southern reaches of Zion the distance between the lowest and the highest layers is approximately 25 miles. In the Kolob Canyons this same sequence is squeezed into a span of less than 5 miles.

Local jointing has produced a set of five east-west running canyons, which are in bold juxtaposition to the general north-south trend of canyons found throughout the rest of the park. These five "finger" canyons appear to have been gouged out of the Kolob Terrace by a giant hand, hence the name.

JOHN P. GEORGE

***In the Kolob Canyons of Zion, the Navajo** Sandstone is uniformly red from top to bottom, unlike exposures in Zion Canyon, which tend to be white on top and red underneath. The iron oxide coloration in the Kolob cliffs has yet to be weathered out because overlying limestone beds have protected the formation from water that would otherwise have begun leaching out the bright red and orange color.*

Isolated mesa tops provide researchers with an invaluable laboratory for the study of evolutionary processes. Like islands in the sea, these inaccessible highlands harbor unique assemblages of plant and animal species. Like other national parks, Zion has been set aside not only for enjoyment and recreation but also for the pursuit of scientific research.

TOM DANIELSEN

Early Mormon pioneers used these drainages as a passage to higher and lower elevations in the seasonal movement of livestock. Humble pioneer cabins remain as evocative reminders of a life filled with harsh and demanding isolation.

The most famous historical figure associated with the Kolob Canyons is John D. Lee, a colorful 19th-century Mormon zealot who was implicated in the infamous Mountain Meadows Massacre of 1857. He lived in the valley below Kolob, where New Harmony is today. Legend has it that before his arrest, he hid among the Kolob cliffs looking for clothes to be hung on a line telling him that the coast was clear to come home. He was ultimately captured and executed by firing squad for his role in this massacre. Lee Pass is named for him.

The five-mile Kolob Canyons road begins at the Kolob Canyons Visitor Center. It then proceeds to climb across the trace of the Hurricane Fault where it abruptly makes an eastward turn up the spectacular canyon of Taylor Creek. Towering above is the highest point in Zion National Park, Horse Ranch Mountain. From its lofty summit it drops nearly 3,000 feet into the precipitous defile of Taylor Creek's north fork. At the Taylor Creek parking lot is the first trailhead where visitors can access the trail to Double Arch Alcove. From here the road continues to climb to Lee Pass, the terminus of a 36-mile network of backcountry trails open to hikers and horseback riders.

Two miles beyond, the road ends at a viewpoint where visitors can survey all five finger canyons. Here visitors can admire the stark contrast of red rock, blue sky, and evergreen forests. In addition there is a half-mile footpath (the Timber Creek Overlook Trail), which leads to a vista of canyons

The trail along the Middle Fork of
Taylor Creek leads to Double Arch
Alcove. This quiet retreat surprises hikers who round a bend to discover a colorful oasis. Not unlike
the more famous Weeping Rock of Zion Canyon, Double Arch Alcove is the result of lateral
water migration along an active spring line, where minerals in solution decorate the walls with
brightly colored streaks. This unique alcove is persistently cool and moist even in the heat
of summer. Plants that otherwise would not be able to grow at this elevation find a hospitable footing
in this environment. (Note the moisture-loving conifer in the left foreground.)

As in architecture, an arch possesses strong self-supporting durability. Notice that the main span of Kolob Arch is rich in red iron minerals. These form strong cementing agents, making the arch even more resistant to erosion than the surrounding rock. Zion contains all three stages of arch development, with Kolob Arch being an example of the latter or mature stage. Double Arch Alcove (page 43) represents initial development of the arch form and the Great Arch (page 14) embodies the middle or intermediate. With a span of 310 feet, Kolob Arch is believed to be the largest freestanding arch in the world.

JOHN ELK III

Hop Valley is a backcountry corridor connecting the main portion of Zion National Park with the Kolob Canyons district. It can only be seen on foot or horseback but is well worth the effort. The flat bottom of this canyon is the result of a lake that was created by a landslide approximately 2,000 years ago. Over time the lake drained away, leaving behind a level surface of sediment that accumulated on the lake bottom.

and mesas to the south. From here on a clear day, one can see all the way to Mt. Trumbull in Arizona near the North Rim of the Grand Canyon, a distance of 125 miles.

The Kolob Canyons has become the premier backpacking area of the park, providing access to wilderness canyons such as La Verkin Creek, Hop Valley, Beartrap Canyon, and the Kolob Arch. Unlike other backcountry zones in Zion, the drainages of the Kolob offer a reliable source of year-round water to overnight hikers. Hikers must obtain wilderness permits at either visitor center before venturing out on multi-day excursions. Aside from backcountry use, the Kolob Canyons is a day use area, with no developed campgrounds.

JEFF GNASS

JOHN P. GEORGE

The Land Between

Not to be confused with the Kolob Canyons, the Kolob Terrace is a separate area of Zion National Park. Like an escalator, the Kolob Terrace Road rises from the low parched desert floor of the Virgin River floodplain to the cool lush forests of a high plateau. Along the way one passes upward through four distinctly different life zones characterized by changing plant and animal species. Atop the plateau at Lava Point, temperatures are as much as 20 degrees cooler than in the main canyon. A small primitive campground is available for those wishing to escape the summer heat of the lower elevations. Lava Point also features a scenic overlook of the Horse Pasture Plateau and the canyons below.

The play of light on the hulking flank of rock known as Job's Head is a high point for travelers along the Kolob Terrace Road. Here the ponderosa pine becomes more predominant as higher altitudes are reached. Repeated lightning strikes on the top of the mesa in the distance have produced fires keeping it relatively treeless. Job's Head is one of many landmarks in Zion possessing a biblical name.

The Left Fork of North Creek flows over the Kayenta shale creating a catwalk series of picturesque cascades. Upstream from here is a narrow slot canyon known as the Subway. Hikers must first obtain a backcountry permit to travel into this rugged corner of the park.

Zion, Parunuweap, Rio Virgin, Mt. Moroni—
these names echo thousands of years
of history spanning several continents.
How appropriate for a place which today
is host to all the citizens of the world.

Those Who Came Before...

The modern-day motorist traveling along Interstate 15 through Southern Utah is in fact traversing an ancient corridor of human migration. This break in the land surface provides a natural passageway that was as obvious to ancient people as it is to contemporary highway engineers. Seemingly isolated, Zion's proximity to this route has invited settlement from a diverse array of peoples.

First among them were the Archaic people, who date back approximately 9,000 years. They hunted small mammals and gathered a variety of plants including the seeds of Indian rice grass, a staple in their diet. They constructed simple baskets and split-twig figurines. The most evocative relics from this culture are large pictograph panels found in Canyonlands National Park. Archaeological remains in Zion are sparse, consisting of baskets and yucca-fiber sandals from a few deeply buried sites.

By about A.D. 750 life became more sedentary, allowing for architectural pursuits and small-scale agriculture. The people of that time are now called Ancestral Puebloans or Anasazi. This group's cultural heart was in the Four Corners region (where Arizona, New Mexico, Utah, and Colorado all meet) east of Zion. Occupying the sparsely populated western fringe of this civilization were the Virgin River branch of the Anasazi. Here they grew corn, squash, and beans along the floodplains of the Virgin River. Their use of small, multi-room masonry pueblos suggests that when farmland was adequate, families would join together in larger groups.

In addition to their architectural achievements, the Ancestral Puebloans also excelled in ceramics. Pottery, both plain and painted, was used for storage and cooking and had value as a trade item. Rock art exists in Zion though hardly in the abundance that it does in the Four Corners region. Petroglyphs and pictographs are protected by the

TOM DANIELSEN

This Ancestral Puebloan *rock carving dates from the Pueblo II period approximately 900 to 1,000 years ago. Petroglyphs, like those pictured here, are chiseled into the rock. Pictographs are images that were painted on rock.*

JOHN P. GEORGE

***Caching food in scattered** locations prevented the loss of an entire harvest due to a single catastrophic event. Granaries like this one were built in locations that were well hidden and inaccessible to rodents. Blending in almost as one with the landscape, Ancestral Puebloan masonry offers an example of organic architecture meant* not *to be seen.*

same strict laws that safeguard all ancient Indian archaeological sites. The basic pattern of small, scattered farmsteads persisted until about 1200, when the Zion area was abandoned, possibly because of a change in climate, resource depletion, encroachment from other groups, or a combination of factors. Ancestral Puebloan art and culture are popular today as icons of the American Southwest.

This harsh desert setting has always challenged its inhabitants. The Southern Paiute had skills that allowed them not only to survive, but actually to prosper. They began to migrate into this area around the year 1000 and became the predominant tribe in the wake of the Anasazi departure. For these desert dwellers, Zion, with its abundance of water, game, and plant resources, was a seasonal sanctuary. During the summer they hunted on the plateaus and when winter came retreated to the desert.

The Paroosit were the band that maintained settlements in the valley of the upper Virgin River. Many of the landmarks in Zion bear Paiute names such as Parunuweap Canyon, Mt. Kinesava, and the Pa'rus Trail. This tribe maintains reservation land in several areas of southern Utah and northern Arizona. In 1997 the National Park Service signed an agreement with the tribe allowing free entry to Zion for religious and ceremonial visits. This agreement acknowledges the time-honored and sacred bond that the Southern Paiute have with the Zion landscape.

Explorers, Trappers, and Settlers

The first recorded visit by people of European descent to southwestern Utah was the Dominguez-Escalante expedition, in 1776. At the same time as the American Revolution, these Spanish padres undertook an adventurous journey in an attempt to find a viable overland route from the settlements at Santa Fe, New Mexico, to those at Monterey, California. Earlier efforts to find a direct route between these Spanish missions had been thwarted by the impenetrable canyons of the Colorado River. Ute Indians led the expedition northwestward through what is now Colorado and then westward to Utah Lake, near present-day Provo. Lacking adequate information regarding a route to the coast, they abandoned their attempt to reach California and redirected southward.

The expedition came within 20 miles of Zion Canyon, making note of Paiute farming and possible sites for future mission settlements. The colonial authorities in Mexico City ignored this remote outpost of the Spanish empire for many years thereafter. A few hunters and traders drifted through. The name Rio de la Virgin, "river of the Virgin," first appeared on colonial maps in the early 19th century.

Fifty years after the Dominguez-Escalante expedition, the region adjoining Zion National Park was explored by a company of men under the leadership of Jedediah S. Smith, one of the many fur traders whose activities make up much of the history of the West during the first half of the 19th century. In his search for pelts, Smith left the outpost of the American Fur Company on the Great Salt Lake in August 1825. In examining the streams along the base of the Wasatch Mountains, he came upon the Sevier River, which he followed southward eventually encountering the Virgin River. Succeeding where the Spanish had failed, Jedediah Smith followed this stream south and eventually to the open country leading to California.

Spanish fur trappers and traders ultimately adopted Smith's route, which became known as the Old Spanish Trail. As far as we can tell, none of these early explorers ever saw Zion Canyon. These travelers diverged little from the most expedient and feasible routes.

Soon after the founding of Salt Lake City, in 1847, Mormon scouts were dispatched southward to establish a settlement corridor to California. Like the Spanish, the Mormons desired a connection to

the coast. This trail is modern-day Interstate 15. One such scout, Nephi Johnson, entered Zion Canyon in November 1858 and is considered the first non-Indian man to do so. The search for new lands suitable for irrigation farming resulted in settlements at Grafton, Rockville, and Springdale, and within lower Zion Canyon. Today these communities still utilize the original irrigation network devised by the Mormon pioneers.

In the early 1870s, a one-armed Civil War veteran named Major John Wesley Powell led two expeditions for the U.S. government through the canyons of the Colorado River. Powell traversed the East Fork of the Virgin River in 1872 and described the slot canyons and Puebloan ruins which would eventually become part of Zion National Park. Powell's description of these canyons and the photographs of J. K. Hillers brought public attention to these scenic marvels. The Powell expedition benefited from the nearby Mormon settlers, who cultivated corn, tobacco, garden vegetables, and fruit trees. The Mormons also grazed cattle and sheep on the high plateaus until 1909, when the area was withdrawn as a national monument.

ESTABLISHING A PARK

In the quarter century following Powell, the area remained very isolated. Its distance from railroads and population centers, the lack of roads, and rugged terrain were barriers not easily overcome.

A government report about this curious landscape was presented to President William Howard Taft, who shortly thereafter set aside, by presidential proclamation, Mukuntuweap National Monument. *Mukuntuweap* was interpreted as a Paiute word meaning "straight canyon." In 1918, the locally unpopular name was changed to Zion and, in 1919, the area was made a national park. Federal control opened the way for making the

Snow adds a vibrant accent to the already brilliant contrast of colors. Relish these moments, for they are short-lived. Snow in Zion Canyon usually melts the same day it arrives. On the plateau it accumulates, and the high country of Zion typically has several feet of snow lasting through the winter and into the spring. Winter in Zion means mild, sunny conditions in some parts of the park and snowy ones in others. Visitors driving in the sunny south entrance are often astonished to see blankets of snow on vehicles exiting from the east. Daggers of ice hanging from moist cliffs necessitate the closure of some trails, but the canyon remains open and hospitable.

GAIL BANDINI

Local visionaries believed that linking Zion, Bryce, and Grand Canyon by roadway would help make tourism a viable industry in Utah. Today tourism is the largest industry in the state, exceeding mining and agriculture combined. When the Zion-Mt. Carmel Highway was completed in 1930, it superseded the scenery as the primary attraction in Zion. It remains a one-of-a-kind monument to brilliant engineering and ambitious construction. Note the crossbedding in the rock that reveals the pattern of the ancient windblown sand dunes.

region more accessible to the masses. In 1923, the Cedar City spur of the Union Pacific Railroad was completed. Within several years the UP built lodges at Zion, Bryce, and the Grand Canyon, stimulating the rapid development of roads.

The Zion-Mt. Carmel Highway was completed in 1930, connecting Zion to points east. This roadway, with its series of steep switchbacks and two tunnels, was an engineering marvel of the time. In the years immediately following its completion, it attracted as many tourists as the landscape itself. Modern visitors are still delighted by the 1.1-mile-long tunnel, with its unusual "galleries." These openings, or windows, in the tunnel wall reveal the deep canyon below.

The Zion-Mt. Carmel Highway represents the era when the automobile reigned supreme as the means to experience national parks. Since that time, increased visitation and concerns about environmental quality have led to support for alternative means of transportation. In 2000 Zion became one of the first national parks to begin operation of a mass transit system. Future historians will note this chapter in Zion's history as a transitional phase in how people access and experience national parks.

Since completion of the major infrastructure, the human story is one of holding out against nature's indifference to the structures of man. Frequent rock falls, floods, and earthquakes have punctuated the history of this park and will continue to do so in the future.

SUGGESTED READING

BRUHN, ARTHUR F. *Exploring Southern Utah's Land of Color*. Springdale, Utah: Zion Natural History Association, 1993.

GARATE, DONALD T. *The Zion Tunnel: From Slickrock to Switchbacks*. Springdale, Utah: Zion Natural History Association, 2001 (revised edition).

JACKSON, VICTOR L. *in pictures Zion: The Continuing Story*. Wickenburg, Arizona: KC Publications, 1989.

WOODBURY, ANGUS M. *A History of Southern Utah and Its National Parks*. Springdale, Utah: Zion Natural History Association, 1997 (revised edition).

SUGGESTED DVD

Zion National Park Towers of Stone, DVD #DV-62, 53 minutes, Whittier, California: Finley-Holiday Films.

In the early 1870s, a
one-armed
Civil War
veteran...
led two expeditions…
through the
canyons of the
Colorado
River.

*T*he severe topography of Zion
*demanded that those who lived
here behave in unusual ways. Separated from timber
resources by the high sandstone cliffs, enterprising men
constructed a cable and pulley system and lowered lumber
off of the forested plateau for use in the towns below. The
ruins of the upper pulley structure on the rim of Cable
Mountain are a monument to pioneer ingenuity.*

*T*he Sentinel stands
*watch over its young
neighbors. The
cottonwood trees in
turn protect all that
thrive in the shade of
their copious canopy.*

Imposing yet hospitable, Zion stimulates an array of emotions. The cliffs envelop us in an embrace that alternately inspires introspection and exhilaration. However it sways us, Zion is always awe-inspiring.

Experience Zion

Enjoying Zion

Meditative refuge, playground, living museum, sanctuary—Zion is all these and more. It attracts casual visitors but also pilgrims who come with a purpose and a plan. Many of them return time and time again, eschewing new destinations for Zion's infinite allure. Children return as adults and find themselves more exuberant than before. Motorists intending to pass through change their plans and stay. Artists are delighted by oddities in color, scale, light, and contrast. These cliffs attract world-class rock climbers searching for the ultimate big wall experience. Some of the routes require great skill and multiple days to complete. Regardless of your intended level of exertion, there are many ways to experience Zion. Allow yourself to be drawn in by the not-so-subtle majesty of this lithic edifice.

JACK OLSON

It's ironic that most hikers pass through Echo Canyon en route to other areas. With its sculptured walls and shadowy recesses, it is a worthy destination in itself. This is the only place in Zion where an established trail leads through a slot canyon.

The Zion Canyon Shuttle System is made up
of two loops. The yellow line represents the Zion
Canyon loop and the orange line the Springdale loop. The Zion Canyon Visitor Center is
the transfer station between the two loops. Ride in from Springdale to avoid parking hassles. No ticket
is required to ride the shuttle. Visitors may step on and off at any of the eight stops.

LIN ALDER

NPS PHOTO BY DENIS DEFIBAUGH

Interaction with
rangers can enhance
your Zion experience.
Park naturalists
present guided hikes,
evening programs,
special shuttle tours,
children's programs, and
a variety of talks and other
activities. Take advantage
of these unique and
enlightening programs.

RICHARD CUMMINS

LIN ALDER

Waterfalls eventually carve canyons. If the hiker on the left were able to return to the same spot in a few million years, he might encounter a scene similar to the one on the right. Water and shade are unexpectedly abundant in these hot and arid environs. Summertime hikers are naturally drawn to the watercourses. Perhaps they are drawn equally by an appreciation for the aesthetics of erosion, the wonder of geology in action.

DAVID WEINSTEIN

Outdoor exhibits help visitors plan a Zion adventure. Whether you have three hours or several days, time spent at the visitor center will assist you in making the most of your stay. Interpretive information and ranger presentations can lead to a greater understanding, and ultimately, a greater enjoyment of the park.

The West Rim Trail is 16 miles of ingenious engineering and unlikely switchbacks. It was paved in order to make it passable for horses and to prevent erosion. Today it is restricted to foot traffic only.

CAROL POLICH

LIN ALDER

With parking hassles no longer a concern, visitors find it much easier to access trailheads and scenic attractions. The propane-powered shuttle system has also helped restore clean air and natural quiet to the canyon. Buses run frequently throughout the day, from before sunrise to well after dark. Bicycles, backpacks, and wheelchairs are welcome.

TEMPLE OF SINAWAVA

Outfitted for an overnight trip, this pair of backpackers traverses slickrock en route to a backcountry camping zone. They watch for loose sand on the surface that can roll out from underfoot and send a hiker reeling. Where no surface debris exists, slickrock is hardly slick at all—rather, like sandpaper, it grips and steadies the sole.

LIN ALDER

The campgrounds at Zion radiate with the energy of people enjoying nature. In these temporary cities a resident's typical day includes a dip in the river, a deer encounter, a romantic sunset, and an evening at the amphitheatre. Located on the broad plains of the lower canyon, the campgrounds occupy the sites of 19th-century Mormon pioneer homesteads—places where backbreaking labor was the order of the day.

NPS PHOTO BY DENIS DEFIBAUGH

Horseback riding adds variety to a Zion visit. Wrangler guides have been leading trips since the 1920s. Tailored for the tenderfoot, these easy to moderate trail rides access a part of Zion Canyon that few others see. This is a chance to experience the canyon at the pace of yesteryear. The horse rides are headquartered at the Zion Lodge.

BRITT PIERSON

FRANK S. BALTHIS

A cyclist takes advantage of the Pa'rus Trail, which connects the visitor center and campgrounds to Canyon Junction, allowing cyclists to avoid vehicle traffic and enjoy some fine scenery along the way. The yellow-blooming rubber rabbitbrush thrives in recently disturbed soils and alongside roads and trails.

LIN ALDER

The term "Color Country"
takes on new meaning
in the fall. Suddenly it is
no longer the chromatic
rocks that are the center of
attention. Overshadowed
most of the year, Zion's plant
life takes center stage in
October and November. First
to change are the aspens
of the high plateau, their
golden leaves providing a
contrast that makes the
neighboring conifers appear
even greener. As cooler
temperatures reach the lower
elevations, the oaks and
maples transform into startling
shades of orange and red.
Finally, fall comes to the floor
of the canyon where
cottonwood, boxelder, and
canyon grape call attention
to themselves in a dazzling
display of multi-hued foliage.
As autumn visitation
increases, no doubt too will
Zion's reputation as a premier
destination for fall color.
Regardless of when you
visit Zion, the experience will
always move and inspire you.

JEFF GNASS

The green and golden tones of the
changing cottonwoods add a
bright and charming air to the upper canyon.
Although it varies from year
to year, late October through early November
is typically the best time
for fall foliage in Zion Canyon.

All About Zion National Park

Zion Natural History Association

The Zion Natural History Association dates back to 1931 when it was formed as the park's principal partner in providing educational material to the traveling public. ZNHA produces 37 publications centered on Zion and the surrounding area. Proceeds from the sales of publications and other interpretive items are donated to the National Park Service for use in education and research. This funding makes possible a variety of activities including Zion's popular Junior Ranger and educational outreach programs, and the printing of the Zion Map and Guide that is distributed free to arriving visitors. This private, nonprofit organization is an indispensable asset to the park and the 2.5 million annual visitors who benefit from high-quality printed information.

ZION SHOOTING STAR
BY LIN ALDER

For more information, contact:
- ZNHA, Zion National Park, Springdale, UT 84767
- Call us at (800) 635-3959 or (435) 772-3264,
- FAX (435) 772-3908,
- or visit our web site at www.zionpark.org

Junior Ranger Program

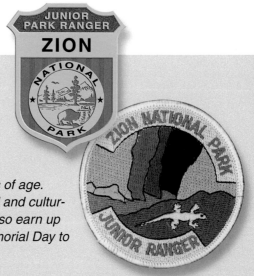

Becoming a Zion Junior Ranger is a fun way for kids to explore Zion National Park while learning how to help take care of Zion and all of our national parks for the future.

Guided Activities—Junior Ranger Explorer:

A summer discovery program is especially for children 6 to 12 years of age. Young explorers have a special chance to learn about Zion's natural and cultural history through games, activities, hikes, and lessons. They can also earn up to two awards, including a certificate/pin and a patch. Available Memorial Day to Labor Day weekends.

Self-guided Activities—Junior Ranger Activity Booklet:

Children ages 6 to 12 can earn a Junior Ranger badge by completing an activity booklet and attending a ranger-led program. Booklets are available at the Zion Canyon and Kolob Canyons Visitor Centers.

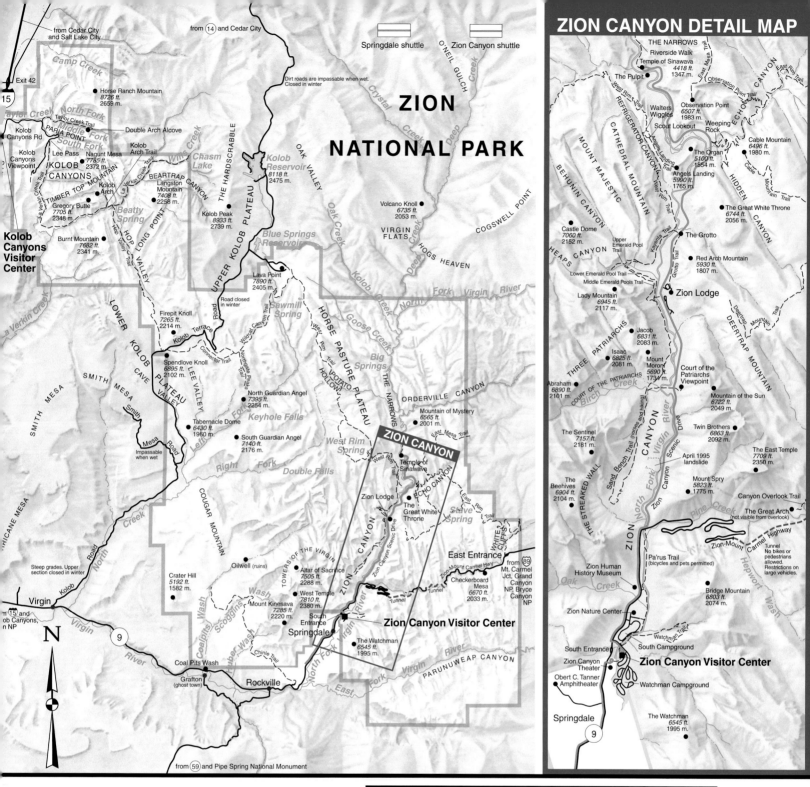

ZION CANYON DETAIL MAP

ZION NATIONAL PARK

Kolob Canyons Visitor Center

Zion Canyon Visitor Center

Zion National Park is located in an area with a heavy concentration of national parks, monuments, and forestlands. It is an ideal launching pad for an exploration of the red rock canyon country of Utah and Arizona. Las Vegas, Nevada, 160 miles south of Zion, has the nearest major airport. Visitors from around the globe find easy highway access, ready accommodations, and an excellent trail system. There are two Visitor Centers to help orient you in your visit. A free shuttle system operates in Zion Canyon from spring through fall. The weather is usually sunny, with summer temperatures commonly exceeding 100° Fahrenheit. Detailed information is available at www.nps.gov/zion.

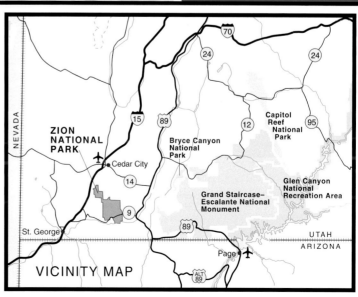

VICINITY MAP

A Look to the Future

With a past stretching back through the Mesozoic, Zion humbles our own existence on this planet. Our time is a trifle when likened to that of these ancient rocks. Yet our existence is hardly insignificant. In our short time we have flourished like no other species. Certainly our success is related to our concern with our own future. We plan for it and we actually influence it.

Zion is currently pioneering new ventures in mass transit and energy-efficient design. The National Park Service believes that these projects will help protect resources while enhancing enjoyment. If these projects are harbingers of the future, it will be poignant that they took place inside one of the earth's most imposing monuments to the past. Perhaps we are not so much humbled by Zion as we are inspired—inspired to leave a beautiful past of our own.

JOHN P. GEORGE

Countless photographers have shot the West Temple from Pine Creek Bridge. Thousands more will capture this image long into the future.

KC Publications has been the leading publisher of colorful, interpretive books about National Park areas, public lands, Indian Culture, and related subjects for over 50 years. We have 4 active series – over 125 titles – with Translation Packages in up to 8 languages for over half the areas we cover. Write, call, or visit our web site for our full-color catalog.

Our series are:

The Story Behind the Scenery® – Compelling stories of over 65 National Park areas and similar Public Land areas. Some with Translation Packages.

in pictures... Nature's Continuing Story® – A companion, pictorially oriented, series on America's National Parks. All titles have Translation Packages.

➜ **NOW, many of our books are available as e-Books.** These vibrant high resolution **e-Books** can be viewed online or downloaded to your PC, Mac and mobile devices. For **e-Book** information, **Visit** this special web site: shop.nationalparkeBooks.com

Voyage of Discovery® – Exploration of the expansion of the western United States.
Indian Culture and the Southwest – All about Native Americans, past and present.

We publish over 125 titles – Books and other related specialty products.

Our full-color catalog is available online or by contacting us:
Call (800) 626-9673, or Write to the address below,
Or visit our web site at www.nationalparkBooks.com
Published by KC Publications – P.O. Box 20039 – Wickenburg, AZ 85358

Inside Back Cover: Crisp air and winter light freshen the Sentinel's façade. Photo by Jeff Gnass.

Back Cover: Unlikely bedfellows, bare rock and green trees commingle well in the unique conditions found in Zion. Photo by John P. George.

Created, Designed, and Published in the U.S.A.
Printed by Tien Wah Press (Pte.) Ltd, Singapore
Color separations by United Graphic Pte. Ltd